MW01490157

The farmer in the dell

A traditional song
illustrated by Lorraine Ellis

The farmer in the dell,

The farmer in the dell,

High-ho, the dairy-o,

The farmer in the dell.

3

The farmer takes a wife,

The farmer takes a wife,

High-ho, the dairy-o,

The farmer takes a wife.

The wife takes a child,

The wife takes a child,

High-ho, the dairy-o,

The wife takes a child.

The child takes a nurse,

The child takes a nurse,

High-ho, the dairy-o,

The child takes a nurse.

The nurse takes a dog,

The nurse takes a dog,

High-ho, the dairy-o,

The nurse takes a dog.

11

The dog takes a cat,

The dog takes a cat,

High-ho, the dairy-o,

The dog takes a cat.

The cat takes a rat,

The cat takes a rat,

High-ho, the dairy-o,

The cat takes a rat.

The rat takes the cheese,

The rat takes the cheese,

High-ho, the dairy-o,

The rat takes the cheese.

The cheese stands alone,

The cheese stands alone,

High-ho, the dairy-o,

The cheese stands alone.